SOMETHING WONDERFUL

BEYOND 2012
THE POSSIBILITIES TO COME

BY
Susan Elizabeth Espinosa

Cover artwork and interior graphics by: Susan Elizabeth Espinosa

Interior Layout: Susan Elizabeth Espinosa

Printed in the USA

For further information visit:

Susan Elizabeth Espinosa at

www.DreamandGoalForIt.com

(818) 377-5196

First Printing: 2012

ISBN [978-0-9711524-0-3]

ACKNOWLEDGMENTS

Jay Smith - Your guidance, humor and gentle assurances gave me the courage to keep seeking. I made you a promise that if I ever wrote a book, I would dedicate it to you. For you Jay, in spirit now, with all my love and gratitude.

*

Daniel Lechowicz - You once told me you were committed to helping me grow through non-cataclysmic means. You did it. I love you across time. Also, thank you for your valuable insights that contributed to the chapter Neptune in Pisces. You are a gifted healer and astrologer.

Steven Espinosa - How lucky am I to have manifested a best friend and soul mate in my brother. If I have to be downwind from cow ass, I'm glad you're beside me.

Bettye B. Binder - A generous teacher in both heart and mind. Your classes offered a safe haven to explore and ask the crazy questions. A true companion through time.

Chere Rae — Supporting me when I thought I was alone. Thank you for your sense of humor and for standing on my bed, burning salt and chanting when I came home. What a sight!

Ralph Kampshoff — My phone husband. So many great and inspiring conversations kept me company in all the many places I have lived. Extra thank you for your time and skill in helping to edit this book.

Jill Standfield — For holding the memory of seeing a scared girl rehearsing for the talent show and calling her confidant. Also, for screaming like teenagers with me at my first celebrity client. You are beautiful and radiant.

Michelle Farris — Right from the beginning you have supported me. I was never more impressed by you then when you jumped out of a plane and never more pleased when you taught your son to speak Starbucks. Anyone you counsel is lucky.

Neal Lidbom — Where are you? I miss your fiery personality. From teaching me to swear in a long list of profanities, my first helicopter ride just for the fun of it and to your marvelous insights from the other side. I can't wait to see you again!

*

With great love and respect to all my Clients. Your willingness to let me share what I have learned from a bumpy ride in life has made the hard times worth it! I am honored to share this journey with you.

DREAM AND GOAL FOR IT!

The book you are holding is a direct result of the
DREAM AND GOAL FOR IT! philosophy:

DREAM IT! FEEL IT! LOVE IT! DO IT!

DREAM AND GOAL FOR IT.COM

Each phrase connects to the *Dream and Goal For It!* teachings of how Universal energy is naturally designed to flow effortlessly through your Soul, Body, Heart and Mind resulting in continuous synchronicities that lead to actualized manifestations.

The material presented has been acquired through the author's personal experience and professional practice as an intuitive life coach.

*What is the Dream inside of you,
waiting to be the Goal manifested?*

www.DreamandGoalForIt.com

December, 2012

As of the final publication of this book, it is 12 days away from December 21, 2012. Most likely you are reading this after the alignment has occurred. Much emphasis has been placed on this specific date for something to happen, when in fact, it is a period of time the date affects. Similar to having graduated from school, the ceremony is important as it represents the culmination of an experience, but it is not the end. However, it is one of three major astrological/astronomical events climaxing in 2012 that will affect us for the next period of time. The question is:

**What will unfold in our lives and in the world
as a result of the
December 21, 2012 event?**

It is a very exciting time to be a witness and a participant to the transformations that will occur. In our personal lives, the shifts are already happening as so many are feeling overwhelmed by the demands of a modern life and a changing economy. We are sensing that something of value is missing from our lives. The astrological and astronomical shifts of 2012 give everyone a chance to live life according to the Laws of Love, ultimately resulting in the good for all. However, as already seen in current events, chaos will arise along with the potential for good. We are all being asked to be responsible for what we think, feel and the actions that result. Why? Because what you create in your life first begins <u>within</u> you. Is it Love or chaos? Joy or pain? Celebrations or sorrows?

With the right understanding, proper instruction on how to handle yourself through this time and the right mindset, what you can achieve has unlimited possibilities. Only <u>you</u> restrict the flow of good available. The alignment offers you an unprecedented opportunity to directly interact with synchronicities. You will draw to you what you feel whether you are balanced or not. You must be willing to learn, adapt to the new information and ultimately be responsible for the change you want to see.

Know that no one today or in our recent history has been alive to experience these events. We are all in this together and need one another to be functioning at our best in order to minimize the potential for chaotic events.

We will soon understand that we are all one people, one planet, one expression of love and what happens to one happens to all. This is why it is important to learn the tools described in this book so that you may clear the way in your Soul, Body, Heart and Mind to be the fullest expression of love possible. You will have access to your full creative potential and be able to clearly see how to actualize what you want and need in life. The more balanced you are the less chaos and stress you will experience.

*With Love,
Susan Elizabeth Espinosa*

DREAM

along with me

and

manifest your GOALS

into Reality

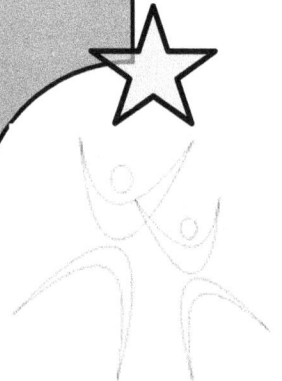

TABLE OF CONTENTS

WELCOME

Something Wonderful began as a series of books I wrote introducing a newly discovered health and healing system I call, *The Seven Keys to Effortless Living*. Through research, client application and personal experience, I recognized that there is a continuously flowing energy exchange from the Divine through every individual. It is an innate part of being human and is accessible within the Soul, Body, Heart and Mind.

This coherence has existed in each one of us since the beginning of time and, until recently, has been hidden from our awareness. When The Seven Keys are operating in unity, their true directive is to awaken your authentic self and align you continuously with synchronistic events that give you access to the power of the Laws of Attraction.

This sacred relationship, as co-creator with the Divine, is humanity's and your intended function in the physical world. *You are here to express your divine identity and to bring forth your unique talents and skills in tribute to the Divine.* You are not meant to shy away from your individuality but to embrace it in order to contribute positively to the world. However, sometimes life, stresses, compromises and expectations make it challenging to freely be your authentic self.

The Keys outline, in a step by step format, how to apply this system into your daily life resulting in an unceasing experience of *Effortless Living*.

> *Don't be confused by the words Divine, Creator, God or Universe.*
> *I am ultimately referring to the all-inclusive, all loving energy*
> *each spiritual system agrees exists in the natural order of life.*

Specifically, The Laws of Attraction state that:

<u>What you *think, feel, visualize, and intend* is what you will attract to you.</u>

and The Seven Keys are what you do BEFORE engaging the Laws of Attraction. This system gives you the ability to be in union with the power of the creative force which was always your birthright.

I have learned both personally and as an intuitive life coach, that this system does require conscious involvement on your part to keep the pathways open in your Soul, Body, Heart and Mind. What you have been given is a gift, but it is up to you to maintain it, and the Seven Keys will teach you how to do this. Knowing how to care for yourself in this way becomes increasingly more important as the uncertainty of the world situation continues to escalate.

*

Additionally, we are entering an extraordinary time of change with events occurring both astrologically and astronomically beginning with the Precession of the Equinoxes. The Precession, which is the result of a wobble in the Earth's axis of rotation, takes approximately 26,000 years to travel through the zodiac. What makes this Precession special is that the Earth and Sun will align with the Galactic Center on December 21, 2012 along with the culmination of the Precessions 26,000 year cycle; a very rare event. Also, in April 2012, the planet Neptune returned to its home base of Pisces beginning the finalization of its current pass through the zodiac which takes 165 years to complete. Collectively we are experiencing simultaneously conclusions of major astrological and astronomical events.

As these events occur and beyond, we should expect to see a rise in upheavals and stress responses as humanity begins to experience the effects of this long awaited evolutionary energy. In the meantime, it is imperative to learn how to function and adapt to the new world emerging and this book will show you how.

The information and techniques I offer are drawn from my personal experience and over 15 years as an intuitive life coach. Additionally, I have a unique astrological profile consisting of a concentration of multiple influences in the intuitive, empathetic and psychic sign of Pisces. Having such an emphasis in these Piscean areas makes me distinctly qualified to understand what is happening during this shift.

In my quest to understand my own suffering and its effect on the Soul, Body, Heart and Mind, I observed that at all times there is a clear, intelligible, loving presence attempting to move through us but is frequently blocked. Just as every car comes equipped with an engine that enables it to perform as designed, the Seven Keys to Effortless Living, when functioning cohesively and as intended, are meant to keep you continuously receiving Universal energy and connecting you with the synchronicities that will guide you in your life.

It was a succession of synchronicities, including the following dream announcing an unprecedented coming *"wave of Love"* connected to the alignment, which led me to understand what extraordinary possibilities are available for us in these chaotic times. I have tried for several years to publish the original series of books explaining my discoveries but was unsuccessful. Though I had the information on the Seven Keys, I realized what was needed was the message *of Hope, Truth and most importantly Love,* which I believe are unfolding side by side with the turmoil of the times.

This book will show you:

> ➤ How to activate and utilize your natural connection to the power of the Universe.

> ➤ How to use this power to reduce stress, increase joy, and be an active co-creator.

> ➤ Why having fun is a necessary component to utilizing the Laws of Attraction.

> ➤ How working with The Seven Keys links you to continuous synchronistic events.

> ➤ How to sustain an optimistic outlook in spite of what is happening.

> ➤ How being your Authentic Self immediately magnetizes to you full Universal support.

Though it may be challenging to see, as the world is clearly experiencing an unprecedented change, I do believe that:

SOMETHING WONDERFUL IS HAPPENING!

DREAM: RATYJA, THE BOY FROM INDIA

A small voice is excitedly repeating the phrase, *"I AM HERE! I AM HERE!"*

I ask, "Who is here?
I hear a male child's voice say,
> *"I am here."* Then a soft giggle fills the air.

"What is your name"?
> *"Ratyja"*

"Where are you"?
> He responds, *"Oh, I have been here since the first release of creation or the beginning of time."*

Suddenly an image appears of a boy who looks to be from India. In the dream, I can see an incredible shimmering, pulsing, iridescent light behind him and I ask,

"Who are you with?"
> *"I am here with the Beloved. Can you believe it? I can see him right now. He is beautiful. He is love. He is a wave of love."*

I knew he meant he was in the presence of the Divine.

I ask, **"Ratyja, there is a phrase I keep thinking about, <u>Something wonderful is about to happen</u>. Do you understand this?"**
> He says, *"Yes, there is about to be a second release of creation….of love. It has not happened since the beginning of creation or since the beginning of time. We are all so excited to see what happens. Love is on its way!"*

Then I could hear a woman's voice telling him to stop talking to me as *"mankind was not ready for this information."*

I had the immediate understanding that this child was purely innocent and joyful in his love for what he called "the Beloved". As children do, he was so excited he needed to tell someone.

My final question was, **"If we are not ready, why are you telling me?"**
> *Because of the love that is coming. It is time. Everyone must know. You must be prepared.*

I awoke stunned with the knowledge that a magnificent opportunity is on its way in the form of a wave of Love emanating directly from the Creator. It will allow all of us to be immersed and transform into its Divine Love Frequency. This has not ever been experienced before and is available only to our generation. We will truly usher in a new age of divinity for countless years to follow and

IT BEGINS NOW

SECTION 1

MAY YOU LIVE

IN

INTERESTING

TIMES

WHAT THE HECK IS GOING ON?

Today's world is very different as people, the economy, the weather and the Earth itself are experiencing dramatic transformations. So many of the structures and support systems we rely on are changing or failing all together.

It has all of us wondering what to expect next and how to prepare for the future.

It is a time when the unknown is confronting us daily and on some level we are all being affected. Analysts cannot predict what is happening to the economy. Financial institutions, designed to protect and grow our wealth, are failing. Scientists are seeing unprecedented changes in weather patterns and increases in Earth changing events. Educational systems are deteriorating as the government continues cutbacks. Religions are having a difficult time due to the continuous exposure of scandals.

In the metaphysical world, intuitive readers, psychics and prediction makers are reporting that it has become difficult to perceive into the future beyond 2012. Many describe a *wall* or *boundary* they cannot penetrate with their intuitive abilities.

As for me, it has never been difficult to see into the future since it happens naturally and involuntarily. It is frequently too much information. Normally, paths of possibilities unfold before me effortlessly; however, beginning in October, 2011, I noticed that seeing intuitively beyond 2012 was becoming challenging.

I now understand that it is for a good reason. There is a unique opportunity coming our way. We are being primed for it by two events happening (or have already happened) in 2012. The first is the astrological passage of the planet Neptune arriving in the sign of Pisces. The second event is on December 21, 2012 when the Sun, Earth and Galactic Center align. This alignment is also referred to as the Mayan doomsday prophecy. Both of these events pave the way for an extraordinary new energy to arrive, which will make available to all, <u>*a direct union with the manifesting forces of the Divine Universe*</u>. This unification has never been experienced by anyone living today. Only a few masters of the past achieved this merging by harmonizing their Soul, Body, Heart and Mind to resonate with unconditional love. Historically, this has been too difficult for the masses to achieve. However, **we are the generation where this harmonization will be possible**. The Mayans knew this and purposefully *directed their prophecies to those of us living today*. Not to warn us of catastrophes, but to prepare us for the revelation that an immense upgrade in the consciousness of humanity will begin with these astrological and astronomical events.

It is hard not to believe that something frightful is indeed approaching. We are all compelled to wonder what might be next. Let us explore the possibility that it may be:

SOMETHING WONDERFUL

NEPTUNE IN PISCES 2012-2026

Coauthored with Daniel Lechowicz, DC

Each planet governs an astrological sign and the planet Neptune rules Pisces. As of April, 2012, Neptune returned to its home position of Pisces and will remain there for fourteen years through January, 2026. When a planet returns to the sign it rules, the areas it affects are impacted significantly.

Neptune is called a *generational planet*. When it is in its home sign of Pisces, it affects an entire generation and will have a very strong influence on the unfolding of events and any shifts in humanity's consciousness.

Together, Neptune and Pisces affect:

- Subconscious
- Oceans
- Dreams
- Intuition
- Paranormal
- Escapism
- Absolute Truth
- Impracticality
- Delusion/Illusion
- Creativity
- Secrets
- Unconditional Love

- Corporations/ Bureaucracies
- Large Militaries
- Financial Institutions
- Politics
- Religions
- The Bigger Picture
- Spirituality
- Leaps of Faith
- Culmination/End of Matters
- Unity
- Timelessness
- Infinity

It takes Neptune 165 years to travel through the twelve astrological signs. Neptune is now concluding its sojourn through the signs when it entered Pisces April, 2012. This is important, for as we proceed, we will see how this ending occurs at the same time the Mayan Calendar is culminating its 5,000 year cycle in December, 2012 within the Precession of the Equinoxes culminating its 26,000 year cycle.

Most Recent Effects of Neptune in Pisces

The last time Neptune was in Pisces was 1848-1863. During this time we experienced:
- ✓ New forms of government emerging and rejecting monarchy rule
- ✓ The American Civil War and the issues of slavery
- ✓ The rise of the Industrial Revolution

Also, in the distant past, many religions arose during Neptune in Pisces:
- ❖ St. Paul began his mission to convert nations to Christianity (46-48 A.D.)
- ❖ Buddhism spread into Japan (552 A.D.)
- ❖ Mohammed received his inspiration and created Islam (610 A.D.)

What to Expect

1. Pisces, being the last sign of the zodiac and the composite of all the astrological signs, symbolizes the culmination of bringing a long era to an end. Neptune connects us to illusions and absolute truth. Collectively, we will be reexamining all that transpired in the last 5,000 years and also within the larger cycle of 26,000 years and seeing:

> ### The Truth of All Matters Rising to the Surface

This includes everything from our understanding of the Universe and the origins of mankind, to the evolution of man and societal structures from the onset to modern times. All will be reviewed as truth breaks through any illusions we have thought were valid.

2. Beginning now, it will be very hard to be secretive or to keep things concealed. All will be known whether directly or indirectly. Anything hidden will come to the surface. Absolute truth will emerge *with or without our cooperation*.

We have already seen the beginnings of great changes in the financial, political and corporate institutions and how they are structured. With Neptune representing absolute truth, these long standing organizations will continue to experience scandals and a demand for restructuring so that they are in alignment with truth. There will be an inclination for a single ruling entity; perhaps the long prophesized One World government.

3. Another affect you may experience will be time anomalies such as time passing unusually fast, confusion surrounding past/present/future events and timelessness as in an extended déjà vu. There will also be an increase in paranormal phenomenon, a rise in unusual abilities and intuition becoming widely accepted.

4. Since Neptune and Pisces together rule religion, spirituality and unity, it is possible that a new spiritual system may emerge which would be a composite of the major religions. The focus will be on the commonality of all, as well as the best of what each represents.

*

Neptune, the Mayan Calendar, the Precession of the Equinoxes

Why is this particular time more powerful than past experiences of Neptune in Pisces? Because this culmination of Neptune's 165 year cycle is happening at the same time the Mayan calendar's 5,000 year cycle is ending along with the previously mentioned 26,000 year cycle. The Mayans knew that the Precession of the Equinoxes would herald a new age for man that would be accompanied by upheavals. So important is this cycle that they wanted to prepare the generation living today with knowledge of what might happen. Their foresight of this time began 5,000 years ago! As these cycles come to a close, a tremendous amount of information will be released into the psyche of humanity. We may not know the full impact of these revelations until 2026 when Neptune enters Aries, the sign of new beginnings. 2026 will be an important year for implementing what we discovered during the years 2012-2026.

Why is This Important?

With Neptune in Pisces bringing all matters to the surface, the alignment of December 21, 2012 will bring forth the last *5,000 years' worth of experiences, for all of humanity as well as the last 26,000 years of evolutionary experiences,* and allow us to see it consciously. We will finally begin to understand that we are all connected like droplets of water in the same ocean. What happens to one happens to all. As this knowledge enters into each person, it will ignite a compassion for healing from the wounds of the past both personally and planetary. However, before healing can occur, chaos may rise first.

How to Work with This Energy

Neptune in Pisces will enable you to see the bigger picture and to understand why the events in your life have happened. Once you see, you are responsible for the change. You may also experience a lack of clarity and focus along with the desire to be idealistic as Neptune in Pisces rules these as well. In order to make practical use of Neptune's idealistic energy, you want to have a system that will stabilize you, provide structure and help discern the truth or *your experiences will become distorted.* We will discuss specifically how *The Seven Keys to Effortless Living* is the system, already inside you, ready to aid you in being grounded, practical and discerning of the truth.

In querying whether or not something is truth or illusion, ask the following:

- *IS THIS FACTUAL? (Be logical)*
- *IS THIS PRACTICAL? (Is this useful?)*
- *IS THIS LOVING? (Free of self-desire or manipulation)*

A good rule of thumb is:

> *BE DISCERNING.*
> *Otherwise, don't get involved.*

REMEMBER:

> *Illusion is a part of the Neptunian experience so test and examine what you have discerned or been told is the truth.*
> *
> *JUST BECAUSE SOMEONE SAYS IT IS TRUE DOES NOT MEAN IT IS!*

THE LOVE FREQUENCY AND THE LOVE WAVE

Each time I connect intuitively in a client session, I am always aware of an all-over presence that accompanies the release of information. This presence feels to me like:

➢ unconditional love
➢ a love for all things
➢ a feeling of unity
➢ a tolerance for things that are normally irritating
➢ a deep compassion for suffering
➢ certainty that all experiences are for a reason

I have named this presence <u>The Love Frequency</u> and with each interaction I am mindful that this energy emanates from the Divine.

Since the Love Frequency arises from the Divine, it is whole, complete, pure, and will instantly transform anything that it is in contact with. Elements of the Love Frequency include:

> **TRUTH, BEAUTY, TRUST, PEACE**

anything less than these elements cannot exist in the same space as the Love Frequency.

What is the Love Wave and What Will it Do?

The Love Wave is something like a restart button. According to the boy Ratyja, 2012 begins a return of the original Divine creative pulse that began life as we know it. He said, *"It has not happened since the first release of creation."* When the Galactic alignment occurs, there will be an opening, like a door, that will allow the Love Wave to flow freely and immerse us in its energy. All forms of life, regardless of where they are located in time, space or matter, will be affected by this wave as it moves through all of creation. It will reunite opposing forces and create a Divine union while simultaneously giving humanity the never-before-opportunity to interact and co-create directly with the Divine.

> **Therefore with the arrival of the Love Wave,**
> **all life everywhere must elevate**
> **to the perfection of unconditional love.**

What Affect Will it Have On People?

I believe we are already experiencing the first of its effects as it draws closer. Keep in mind, truth is emerging in areas of your life that need balancing so it may be disruptive.

Clients report deep and often sudden changes happening in their physical, emotional and spiritual life. Perhaps some of these you may also be experiencing:

- Loss of job
- Diminished income
- Health issues
- Sudden loss of loved ones
- Seeing spiritual phenomenon
- Increase in psychic awareness
- Lack of sleep or disturbing vivid dreams
- Break up of relationships or feeling unable to leave a relationship

Why All the Chaos?

Our ability to create begins with an expression of emotion. Humanity has not yet learned how to respond appropriately to our more difficult emotions such as fear, anger and sorrow. The result, _whether we are conscious of it or not_, is _we will manifest from our emotional state_. At this time, humanity is quite literally creating reality from the collective unconscious of fear, which creates the very chaos we see happening. Until we learn how to manage our emotions, the events we are manifesting will become more intense.

**I believe that many intuitive readers are having a difficult time seeing beyond the current time stream because <u>for the first time in mankind's history</u> we are collectively co-creating our reality. Sadly, we are manifesting from a feeling of fear and not love as the Divine had intended.**

Though this may seem disturbing, keep in mind that before a lasting change can happen, the systems that are in place promoting disharmony, not conducting business truthfully or being unloving must be dismantled.

This is why _you_, the individual, matters. The more you CLEAR THE FEAR then you will not _Create What You Hate_. You do have magnificent power in a way you may never have understood. This will become clearer as we discuss the Seven Keys to Effortless Living and the importance of Following the Fun.

**"What can I do?"**

**"How can just one person make a difference?"**

These are questions I often hear repeated by my clients. Love is an energy that is whole and complete. When Love comes into contact with polarity, that polarity will transform into oneness.

If that polarity is in the expression of an individual personality, the Love energy will transform the personality into an expression of an authentic self.

This was the original intention of the Divine. That we express ourselves as true reflections of divine love and not the fear based reactionary personalities so many have become. We are not the person we adapted into being as a result of life circumstances.

By actively uncovering and facing your fears, confronting what has made you angry, disappointed, etc. you neutralize this energy and become a conduit for the pure love of the

Creator to flow through you granting abundance, peace and joy. As you feel this continuous presence, it will affect those around you by uplifting them to new possibilities which can ultimately have an effect on the world.

What May Happen – A Summary

With Neptune now in Pisces, we are beginning to see an emergence of deep truth arise in the restructuring of our world systems as well as transforming the unconscious, collective mind of humanity. When the alignment of December 21, 2012 happens, it will be as if a door opens to the center of our galaxy allowing the Love Wave to move through all of creation.

As this surge of Love Frequency washes over all of existence, we will be required to rise to the level of unconditional love that so far only a few masters of our distant past have accomplished. It is not known yet if the effects of the wave will be immediate or a slow revelation but one thing is clear...*this event will leave nothing untouched as we begin to experience the unifying of heaven and earth*.

What Can You Do?

What follows are teachings from *The Seven Keys to Effortless Living* which prepare you for this event as it unfolds in your life.

The Keys are:

KEYS 1 - 3
• *BE YOURSELF*
• *FEEL YOUR FEELINGS*
• *BE HAPPY*

KEYS 4 - 7
• *SOUL (Guidance from the Universe)*
• *BODY (Receives Insights from Your Soul)*
• *HEART (Connected to Your True Self)*
• *MIND (Organizes Body, Soul, Heart Information)*

Learning how to work with The Keys will give you the foundational support needed to participate in these times. There are very specific functions of the Soul, Body, Heart and Mind that we have not been able to understand. Each has its own unique function that when used properly, allows for a clear pathway of connection between you and the Divine. There are also specific emotional and mental states that are integral to being able to fully apply the true spiritual purpose of the Keys.

So let's begin.

SECTION 2

THE ORDER
OF
ENERGY FLOW

LIFE WAS NOT MEANT
TO BE A STRUGGLE!

Did you know you have a natural ability *within you* to connect with Universal energies so you can manifest the life of your dreams? Have you attempted to use techniques connected to the *Laws of Attraction, Manifestation* and *Synchronicity* and have not been satisfied with the results? Perhaps you have created vision boards or recited affirmations and still feel as if something is missing?

One of YOUR inherent gifts is the ability to be a co-creative partner with the Universe and to utilize, <u>at will</u>, the Laws of Attraction but first you must awaken and activate The Seven Keys to Effortless Living.

<u>Why is That?</u>
The **Seven Keys** are what you *must do BEFORE* you use any manifesting technique. Utilizing the **Keys** will give *you* the power to create with greater accuracy.

Once you understand each of the **Keys** and how they work together you can:

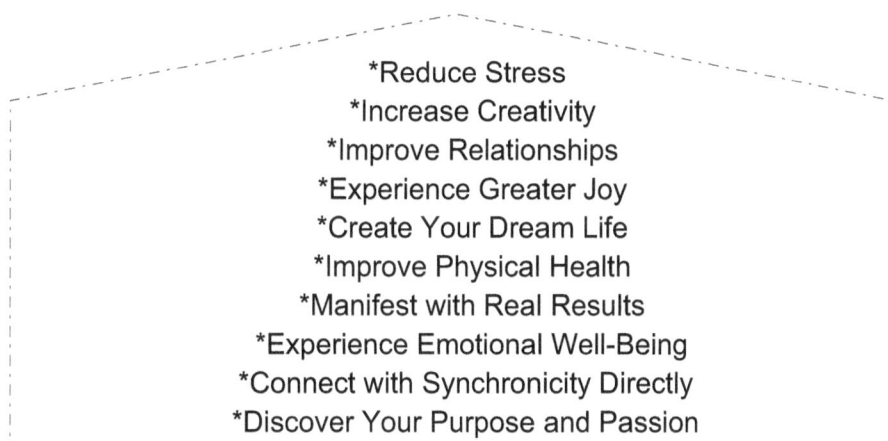

*Reduce Stress
*Increase Creativity
*Improve Relationships
*Experience Greater Joy
*Create Your Dream Life
*Improve Physical Health
*Manifest with Real Results
*Experience Emotional Well-Being
*Connect with Synchronicity Directly
*Discover Your Purpose and Passion

<u>*WHAT ARE THE SEVEN KEYS TO EFFORTLESS LIVING?*</u>

1. *Be Yourself*
2. *Feel Your Feelings*
3. *Be Happy*
4. **SOUL** *(Receives Guidance from the Universe About Your True Self)*
5. **BODY** *(Receives Insights from Your Soul)*
6. **HEART** *(Translates Insights Into Hopes, Wishes, Dreams)*
7. **MIND** *(Organizes Body, Soul, Heart Information Into Actionable Steps)*

🔑
THE KEYS

1. **Be Yourself:** Do you experience unusual aches and pains? Tired? Dissatisfied? *These types of imbalances are indications of not living as your TRUE authentic self.* When living as your true self, you continually draw balanced energy from the infinitely abundant Universe. **Living as your true self aligns you directly with the Universe and all of its manifesting potential.**

2. **Feel Your Feelings:** They are your built-in guidance system. Have you felt uneasy when making a decision? Maybe you dislike someone you just met and don't know why? These are your feelings directing you towards what is right for you!

3. **Be Happy:** Sound too simple? Happiness is your natural state of being. You may have stressful experiences, but you can choose to return to happiness at any time much the way children do. They process their feelings immediately and then return to joy.

The next four **Keys** are:
THE FUNDAMENTAL FOUR

4. **SOUL** receives guidance for you from the Divine Universe. This knowledge is transmitted to your Body.

5. **BODY** receives insights about you from your Soul. Sometimes this information is experienced as pain, illness or injury. Learn to decode the language of the body to restore balance and be open to your…

6. **HEART,** which translates Soul guidance into hopes, wishes, dreams and feelings. This information is given to your…

7. **MIND,** which is like a computer and can sort and organize your hopes, wishes, dreams and feelings so you can take action and *manifest what you desire.*

*Using the Keys
increases your ability to
manifest more accurately*

Do you remember the childhood game *Telephone?* You begin with a sentence that is whispered to several people down the line. When the last person receives the message, they say it aloud and everyone laughs because the sentence has changed. *You* are similar to the line of people in the telephone game. Your Soul communicates pure guidance to you but by the time it has traveled through a blocked Body, Heart and Mind it has changed.

For Instance:

- When you *suppress your feelings* it may affect the function of your **BODY** and prevent you from understanding your **SOUL**'s guidance.

- If you work at a job you dislike *(not being yourself)*, you are not living the hopes and dreams of your **HEART**.

- If you use your **MIND** to focus on fears *(not being happy),* instead of taking action on your **SOUL**'s guidance, then…

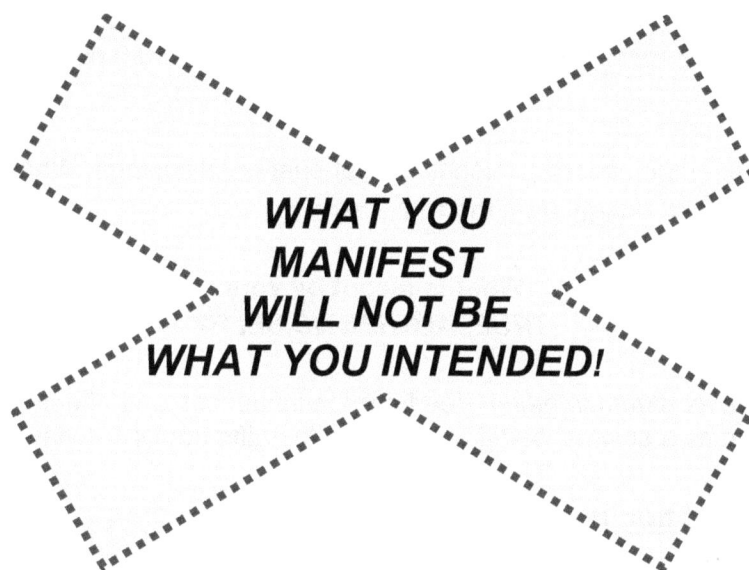

*WHAT YOU
MANIFEST
WILL NOT BE
WHAT YOU INTENDED!*

🔑1 BE YOURSELF

****

*"It takes courage to grow up and
become who you really are."*

~e.e. Cummings

****

That is your true, *authentic* self, which is free of past conditionings. When living as your true self, you continually draw energy from the Universe.

**What is meant by your
TRUE, AUTHENTIC SELF?**

1. Who you are as a *human being,* free from the influences and effects of past events.
2. Who you are as a *spiritual being,* expressing the gifts the Divine gave you.

What are Past Conditionings?

This is an important question to consider because:

> *Who you think you are is largely the result of
> adjustments and compromises you made
> when you determined that
> being your true self was not safe.*

For Example: An imaginative child enjoys creating stories. It would be best to encourage this expression through writing, art, play etc. However, the child is told to focus on academics and adjusts to this conditioning while suppressing the authentic self. This adjustment is never forgotten by the Soul, Body, Heart and Mind and in later years, it may appear in life as:

```
              illness
   low self            aggression
   esteem

   grinding                exhaustion
    teeth

 inability to                overly
 maintain job              emotional

  forgetfulness              weight
                            gain/loss

   accident        hormonal      skin
    prone         inbalance   disorders
```

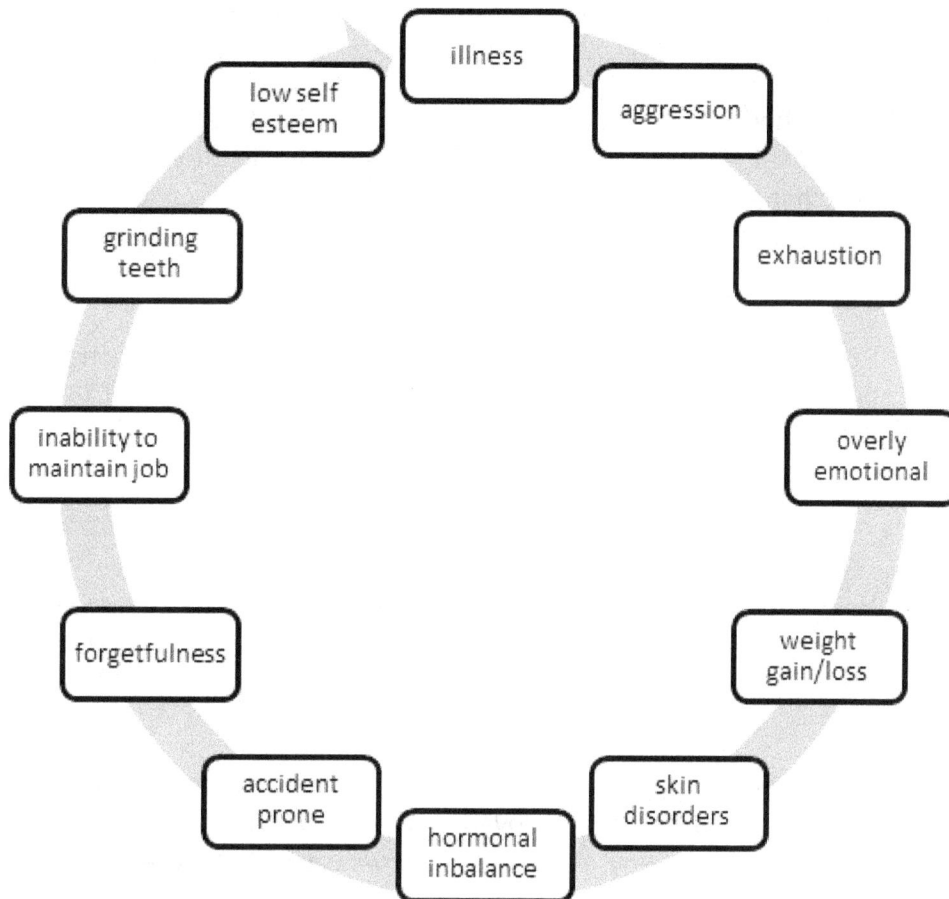

How Do You Begin to Eliminate Conditioning?

First, identify something from your past that you really enjoyed doing. It might be riding your bike, coloring, playing with your pet, singing, being outdoors, dancing, competing in sports, being secretive, going on adventures, doing magic tricks, playing dress up. The possibilities are endless.

Try This: Having trouble recalling your past? Here are three ways to stimulate your memory:

1. Look at pictures from your past. Is there a common theme? *Look at what you are wearing. What objects are in the background? Are you playing with a certain toy? What did your room look like?* Select pictures where you look happy or engaged in some activity.

2. Watch a television show you used to enjoy. There is a reason the subject matter interested you. *Did you like Action? Adventure? Romance? Mystery? Drama? Science Fiction?*

3. Listen to music from a particular time in your life. Music has an immediate way of bypassing the rational mind and stimulating the subconscious, where we store our memories.

Once you have established a memory, find a way to incorporate an aspect of that memory into your life today. Experiment with how to bring that feeling alive again for you in current time. This is how you begin to eliminate conditioning!

Examples:

- You discovered you enjoyed being with your friends and figuring out how to build things. *Go to a hobby store and buy a car or airplane model; build Legos with your kids; take a class from a home improvement store; volunteer for Habitat for Humanity.*

OR

- You enjoyed dressing up and playing pretend. *Go see live theater; volunteer your time to a local repertory company; take a creative writing course.*

These are a few suggestions to begin connecting with the memories of your true self and incorporating the experiences you once loved into your current life. Ultimately, you are connecting with the Universal energy of *Love* and allowing that love to express itself through your new-found authenticity. When you are able to sustain a continuous flow of Love, you will experience immediate improvements in your manifesting ability as you will be in harmony with Divine Universal energies.

⚷ 2 FEEL YOUR FEELINGS

****
"There is no logical way to the discovery of these elemental laws.
There is only the way of intuition,
which is helped by a feeling for the order lying behind the appearance."
                                                          ~Albert Einstein
****

Many people would rather not feel their feelings. How do we know this? Take a look at the endless commercials trying to sell the benefits of the latest pill. Medication is necessary in some cases. *You know when you need it* and are grateful for it. But there are many drugs available today that are not necessary.

Feelings are a natural, normal and an essential part of being human. When you give control over your emotions to pharmaceuticals, you may temporarily suspend feeling unpleasant but you are simultaneously *disconnecting yourself from your natural ability to create joy, passion and happiness in your life.*

Feel your feelings. They are your natural guidance system. When you suppress your feelings, it brings imbalance to the body, inhibiting your ability to manifest.

Childhood Misunderstandings

Our feelings start very early in life. Beginning with our newborn experience of expressing base emotions in order to be fed, kept warm and cleaned; how we feel about our environment and the people in it, is determined when we are quite young, often preverbal.

As stated in the quote above, *the order lying behind the appearance* also refers to the early awareness and decisions we made when we determined our needs were not going to be met. As we grow up and begin to use language to express ourselves, the early childhood revelations are sent to the background, encased in our feelings rarely to be understood by the adults we become. However, those original understandings of how life was going to be are now at the core of ALL of our interactions like the wizard behind the curtain. For instance, if you had a non-attentive parent and had to wait to get your basic needs met, you may experience life in a constant state of panic you cannot account for. In your Body, you may experience breathing related problems since panic requires the Body to respond with an increase of energy and produces the flight or fight response. In your Mind, you may have constant thoughts of fear manifesting in a lack of money or stability in your life. These early childhood feelings are in charge of your adult life and affect your ability to make whole, well thought out decisions.

The Divine did not give you feelings to torment you. Your feelings connect you directly to the Universe. When you manifest, you draw or attract what you want *through your feelings.*

How does this work? You send a feeling signal out to the Universe and it tracks your manifestation back to you, like a homing beacon. This is why it is essential to clear yourself of any blockages obstructing the Universal energy from flowing through you and magnetizing to you what you have desired in your manifestation. Working with Keys 4-7, *The Fundamental Four (*Soul, Body, Heart and Mind) will help you do this.

It is also important to know how and when to use your feelings.

> There is *right action and right timing* connected to expressing your feelings.

We are not taught how to recognize right action and timing. This is why feelings are misunderstood or labeled as bad. This is easy to remedy with help in the form of counseling, books and workshops, designed to educate you about emotions and how to interact with them appropriately.

Benefits of Feeling Your Feelings:

- *Natural guidance system*
- *Connects you to intuition*
- *Informs you when there is an imbalance in your body*
- *Supports you in making beneficial decisions*
- *Warns you of danger*
- *Allows you to feel love*
- *Tells you when to stop or proceed*

With all these benefits connected to feelings, it is easier to understand the importance of allowing yourself to be fully aware of your feelings.

REMEMBER:

When you suppress what you feel,
you can create imbalances in your Body,
which will limit your ability
to manifest what you desire most!

*

For a fascinating video on the power of feeling to heal deadly diseases, visit my website www.dreamandgoalforit.com and see a video with author Gregg Braden lecturing on his book Divine Matrix. It shows a woman with bladder cancer being healed, in less than two minutes, by a group of practitioners who have been trained to feel a very specific feeling in their heart coupled with the intent that she is already healed. The video shows, in real time, via a sonogram, the image of the tumor as it shrinks.

⟨🔑 3⟩ BE HAPPY

Be Happy – It's a choice! Happiness is your natural state of being. It is normal to respond to stressful situations, but you can always return to happiness, just as children do. What makes it difficult to sustain is our desire to hold on to people, places and things that may no longer benefit us.

Being able to let go, release, surrender to your natural state of happiness is what is required to Be Happy. This is an instinctive state of living for young children. They feel their feelings and, when ready, they return to joy. They have not been taught that happiness is difficult to achieve.

> **Jesus said, "*Become like little children in order to enter the kingdom of Heaven.*"**

Know It Is **Your Right** To Experience A Joyful Life
And Within Your Power
To Reset Yourself To That Feeling At Any Time.

*

Try This: Observe children and watch how they move from one emotional state to another. They *Feel Their Feelings*, sometimes very intensely, and in a short amount of time, they return to their authentic self, which lives in a natural energy of happiness.

How do they do this? Because ***no one has told them that it is not possible!*** Since they are young, they do not have a history of experience and conditioning telling them they cannot be happy.

They can teach us that:

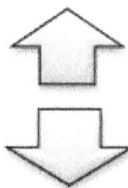

⬆ ***Being Happy is a Choice**

⬇ ***Life is Not Meant to be a Struggle**

Don't Worry, Be Happy

When you worry, you deplete yourself of the energy needed to maintain balance in your Soul, Body, Heart and Mind and disconnect yourself from your natural ability to manifest.

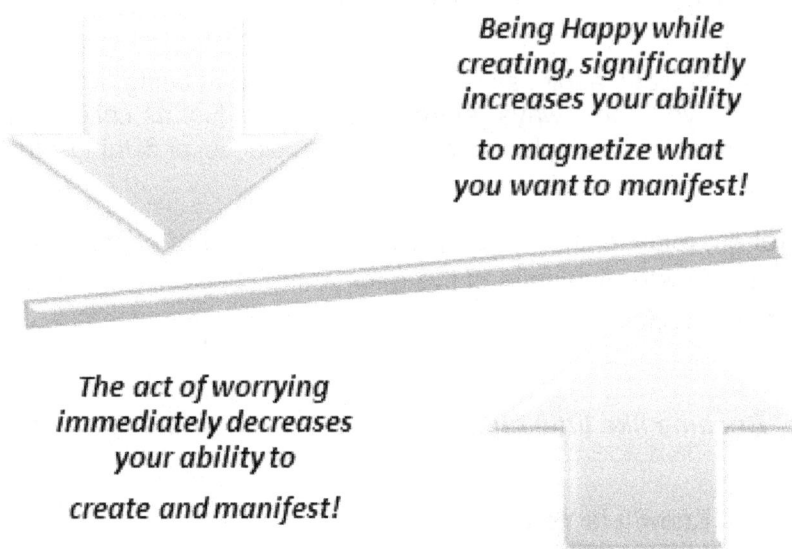

Being Happy while creating, significantly increases your ability

to magnetize what you want to manifest!

The act of worrying immediately decreases your ability to

create and manifest!

You cannot worry and create positively at the same time. Feeling happy directs your creative power towards manifesting good.

DO NOT CONFUSE WORRYING WITH LOVE
Worrying decreases energy and Love increases energy.

What to Do Instead: If you are worried about someone you love, try not to focus on what harm may come to them. Instead, connect with a joyful time and re-live that time in your Mind. This energy will be received as uplifting and will elevate them above their problems and increase their ability to create solutions.

*

Now you know happiness is part of your natural authentic self! Keep in mind that it is normal to respond to stressful situations. However, you can choose to Feel Your Feelings *even if they are unpleasant* and when ready, return to your center of joy. By blocking or suppressing your feelings, you delay your ability to return to balance.

It is your right to be happy. To be anything less is not fulfilling your Divine mission. As you look around the evolving world, it is obvious that *Happiness, Love, and Compassion* are desperately needed. By embodying *The Seven Keys to Effortless Living* you can live a more satisfying life while simultaneously showing others how to do it for themselves.

Someone has to begin. *Is it you?* Even though you see suffering in the world, know *there is something YOU can do about it.* Create a better world *now, today,* through being the example of how to:

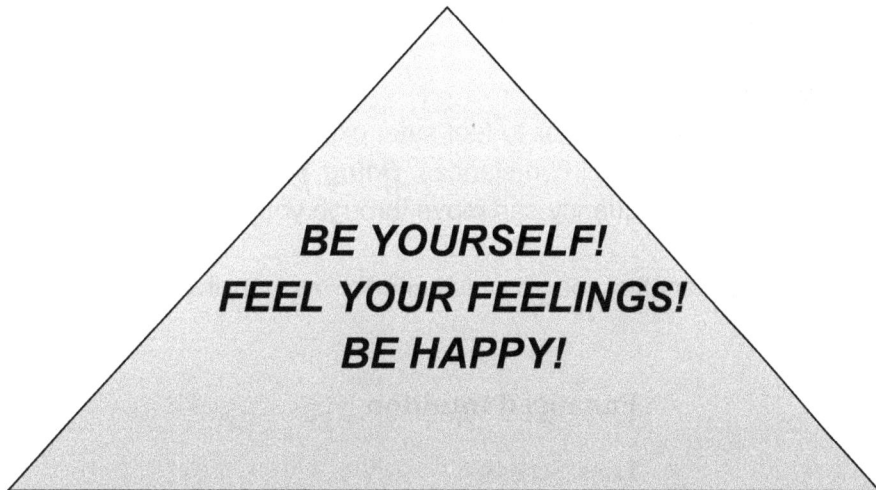

*BE YOURSELF!
FEEL YOUR FEELINGS!
BE HAPPY!*

THE FUNDAMENTAL FOUR

🔑4 *KNOW YOUR SOUL*

"The Soul's emphasis is always right."

~Ralph Waldo Emerson

The Soul emanates from the Divine and it contains the knowledge of your true, authentic self, which is passed onto the Body. When you are **Being Yourself**, *the first of the* **Seven Keys,** you are in a direct dialogue with the information contained within your Soul.

What Does it Mean to Be Yourself?

Oftentimes, in order to be accepted or to feel safe, experiences from your past taught you to retreat from your natural reaction to circumstances. **Being Yourself** is living from your authentic place of truth where the Love Frequency can move through you continuously.

Here are a few of the benefits you may experience as you live according to your Soul's guidance:

- ✓ **Enhanced Intuition**
- ✓ **Less Stress**
- ✓ **More Energy**
- ✓ **Increase in Confidence**
- ✓ **Youthful Appearance**
- ✓ **Increase in All Forms of Abundance**

The Soul knows your true self and will continuously impart this knowledge through the Universal language of:

```
         ┌──────────┐ ┌──────────┐
         │          │ │          │
         │ ARCHETYPE│ │  TONE    │
         │          │ │          │
         └──────────┘ └──────────┘
         ┌──────────┐ ┌──────────┐
         │          │ │          │
         │  COLOR   │ │ FEELING  │
         │          │ │          │
         └──────────┘ └──────────┘
```

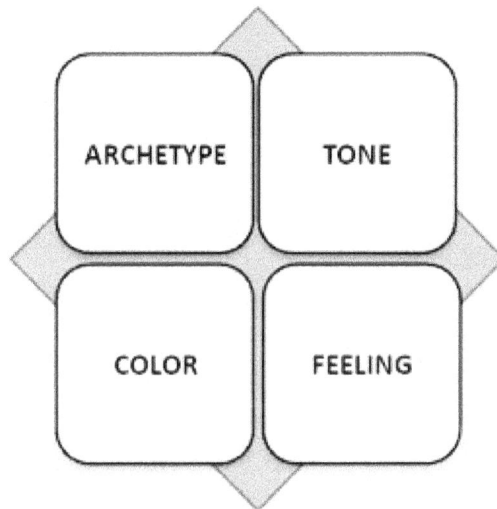

How Does This Work?

Archetype
A symbol that implies a meaning
(a store logo communicates instantly its identity without using words.)

Tone
A frequency or sound that the body responds to and can disrupt or enhance the flow of
Universal energy

Color
Evokes an instinctive reaction; mood producing; may determine health status

Feeling
When you combine an archetype with tone and add color, it will evoke an immediate feeling
response in the Body

This combination is as powerful as any language in its effectiveness to communicate directives to you and is widely used by marketers and the media to manipulate you into buying their products or services.

Why is it Important For You to Know How Soul Communicates?
Once you are aware, you begin to see how this information is used in our society for control. When *you* are affected by these exploitations, *your* energy is being used to fulfill what someone else wants to manifest! This same energy, *when kept for yourself,* gives you greater power to create what YOU want in your life, for your loved ones and the world!!

Try This: Low on energy? Here is an example of how to use Archetype, Tone, Color, and Feeling to manifest physical energy.

Archetype:	*Image of the Sun*
Tone:	*Create a happy sound you like*
Color:	*Yellow/Orange*
Feeling:	Combine all three, use in a visualization such as:

❖ Imagine a battery filling with yellow/orange energy of the sun while emitting the happy sound you selected

❖ Pumping gas into your car which represents your body and seeing yellow/orange balls of sun energy filling the tank and raising it to the full mark while you sing a song you enjoy

❖ Direct yellow/orange sun shaped smiley faces towards your adrenal glands while toning a sound that is pleasing

NOTE: It is best to use the following colors as they correspond to the Body's natural energy centers (chakras).

VIOLET

INDIGO

BLUE

GREEN

YELLOW

ORANGE

RED

BROWN

🔑 5 *KNOW YOUR BODY*

```
***************************************************************************
```
*"The Body's innate intelligence
is always right."*

~Daniel Lechowicz D.C.
```
***************************************************************************
```

As health insurance costs soar and our medical systems become less effective, it is vital for you to understand the language of your own Soul/Body connection and what *your* particular imbalances are communicating. Curious about what your Body is saying? For a quick visual scan, stand up and observe the following in yourself:

Are your feet turned out when you stand?
You are searching for your identity.

Does your back hurt?
You are not feeling supported.

Shoulders slumped?
Are you worried about the future?

Sore throat?
What do you need to say?

SOUL & BODY

Your Body receives guidance or *energy information* about you from your Soul and, like a book; you can learn to *"read"* the contents by understanding that each part of your body has an innate higher meaning such as:

Legs:	*Walk you forward in life*
Hips:	*Represent your identity*
Back:	*Your support systems*

Your Soul transmits guidance nonverbally and *directly into your Body*. Your Body receives this knowledge or *energy information* as aches, pains, illness and sometimes injuries which can cause blockages; therefore it becomes important to learn how to decode the guidance into useful information. When you know how to decode your Soul's guidance, as experienced through your body's imbalances, you can *eliminate stress, restore physical vitality and experience more joy*.

You are unique and there are many combinations of imbalances that will tell *your* particular story. Know that the imbalances provide an immediate way of detecting when you have strayed away from your Soul's directives and your Heart's desires.

Example: If someone broke their leg and injured their back, Soul may be communicating to them their *fear of moving forward in life and not being supported.*

BODY & MIND

The Mind does not know the difference between **what is real and what is imagined** therefore, what you visualize, daydream or think about, can have a *direct* impact on your Body *because Body follows thought.*

It is very important to be clear in your thoughts when manifesting.

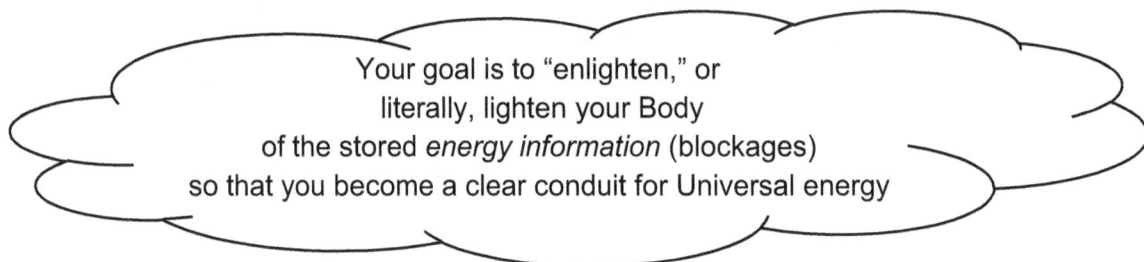

> Your goal is to "enlighten," or
> literally, lighten your Body
> of the stored *energy information* (blockages)
> so that you become a clear conduit for Universal energy

How Does This Effect Manifestation?

When this energy moves through you unimpeded, you are able to create *in partnership with Universal forces!*

What You Think About Has A
Direct Impact On How Your Body Responds To LIFE.

*

Recent times have been especially challenging as we have dealt with dramatic changes to our sense of safety. The reality is you do not have control over what is occurring in the world, *but you do have power over what you think and how you react.*

When you worry, it sends signals to your body that you are in danger and activates your flight or fight response. Look at the list below. Are you experiencing any of these indicators of stress and worry?

- Health problems
- Memory difficulties regardless of age
- Exhaustion
- Lack of joy or enthusiasm
- Feeling of trudging through the day
- Difficulty maintaining daily routines
- Hopelessness
- Feeling scared and impending doom
- Difficulty sleeping

The intensity of these symptoms can be reduced by balancing yourself with experiences of fun and joy.

> **When your Soul, Body, Heart, and Mind
> are filled with the energy experienced
> from having fun, you minimize
> your stress responses.**

Additionally, research on hormones is highlighting the different affects it has on men and women. Author John Gray, a pioneer in the field of male/female relationships, has written about this in his latest book, <u>Venus on Fire, Mars on Ice</u>. Studies show that men require challenging, problem solving situations in order to release testosterone, which in turn lowers their stress. On the other hand, women require nurturing experiences, no time pressures and the opportunity to talk in order to release their stress relieving hormone, oxytocin. When we know what is required of us biologically, we can be proactive in reducing our stress and supporting our bodies in receiving and sustaining joy.

Something Else to Consider

Conditioning from your past can have an effect on how you respond to life, such as:

- **Parental Teachings** – Since there is no formal training to be a parent, teachings are usually a combination of common sense and what was taught through the generations. *There is a reason children go through a rebellious stage*; instinctively they know some of the lessons can be out of balance with their natural selves because what was important to earlier generations may no longer apply.
- **Educational Systems** – The same information has been taught for many years and is based on memorizing and repeating vs. teaching how to think on your own and problem solve.
- **Societal Beliefs** – What is acceptable to do or achieve in order to fit in, such as when to marry, have children and buy a house.
- **The Times in Which You Grew Up** – Each generation has a different energy or mission to express. This will influence how you perceive the experience of fun.
- **Group Consensus** – We all have the need of belonging to a community. If ideas are not in alignment with the group intention, one risks isolation.
- **Ancestral Influences** – Such as the passing down of rituals, codes of conduct, beliefs on how to survive. In my observations, the collective body of ancestral experience is encoded and passed down through your DNA.

- ☆ *FOR INSTANCE:* A client's grandparents died in war and she was taught to keep their memory alive by participating in rituals that activated the ancestral memory of grief and terror. This repetition of ritual, in order to mourn (not celebrate) their life, kept her trapped and connected to a past <u>she had not actually experienced</u>. She had frequent panic attacks and a continuous feeling of doom she could not account for. Why?

> **Your Body, like your Mind,
> does not know the difference between
> what is *actually* happening and
> what is memory or imagination**

Keep This In Mind: Conditioning can be challenging to change, but you can influence the extent to which it affects your responses.

So, if you worry about the future or are angry about the past, your body will respond with the flight or fight response which releases hormones created to handle emergencies because <u>your body thinks it is happening NOW</u>.

Try This: I Love You, I Am Sorry and Thank You

In Dr. Masura Emoto's book, <u>Messages in the Water</u>, his research shows that when either destructive or positive messages are aimed at water, it changes the cellular structure. Knowing that the human body contains a considerable amount of water, you can imagine how damaging or healing the right words can be on the health of your body. Since the body receives as "real" the words you say to yourself throughout the day, you can literally reduce or restore your health and vitality for life by what you think or say.

*

There is a healing technique that uses words and feelings to heal imbalances in the body. The technique is simple. Direct your attention to that which you want to restore balance to such as a sore throat. Place your hands in that area and say:

"I am Sorry. I Love You. Thank You."

When I work with this technique, I am more specific by first identifying the Soul/Body meaning behind the area affected such as your throat expresses your ability to communicate.

<u>Say the following:</u>

> *"I am so sorry that you are hurting and that it has taken getting this painful sore throat for me to pay attention.*
>
> *I really love you for being willing to show me where my imbalance is occurring and giving me the chance to heal it.*
>
> *Thank you from the bottom of my heart for what you are doing."*

I have used this technique successfully reducing or eliminating pain but you may still need to process the imbalance or physical side effects out of your system.

Saying the words, *coupled with true feeling*, is what allows for healing to occur. Everyone needs to hear these words. We have all been wounded and need to be acknowledged. These words connect you to the Love Frequency. In fact, because you are human, you are designed to require the Love Frequency to sustain life as much as you need to eat and drink.

(🔑 6) *KNOW YOUR HEART*

"Where your treasure is,
there will your heart be also."

~ Bible

And what a treasure it is!

A famous princess once said, *"Only do what your Heart tells you."* Your Heart contains guidance from your Soul and is recognizable as your hopes, wishes, dreams and feelings for what you want to experience in your life as your true self. When you connect with your Heart, it acts as a homing beacon, continuously guiding you. This is what is meant by **Follow Your Heart.**

Of the **Fundamental Four,** the Heart is the most challenging for many to connect with, since one's *"Heart's desires"* may seem selfish or impossible to achieve.

Did you know that you feel through your Heart? It is not so shocking then, to learn that the rate of Heart disease, especially among women, is increasing. Also, the denial of the Heart has a direct effect on your nervous system. Have you ever wondered why mood stabilizers have become so popular in this country? We are a nation disconnected from our Hearts.

Author, Gregg Braden, in a lecture from his book, <u>Divine Matrix</u>, says:

> *"When we have a feeling in our heart, we are creating electrical and magnetic waves inside of our bodies that extend beyond our bodies into the world around us. And what is so interesting, is that the research shows that those waves extend not just one meter or two meters but many, many kilometers beyond where our heart physically resides.*
>
> *When many people get together with one feeling, many hearts together creating one feeling, it can change the world. It is only a miracle until we understand the science, then it becomes a powerful internal technology."*

Gregg Braden's in depth studies have uncovered fascinating information on how intimately the physical heart is connected to our emotional body response.

How Do You Discover And Connect With What Your Heart Wants?

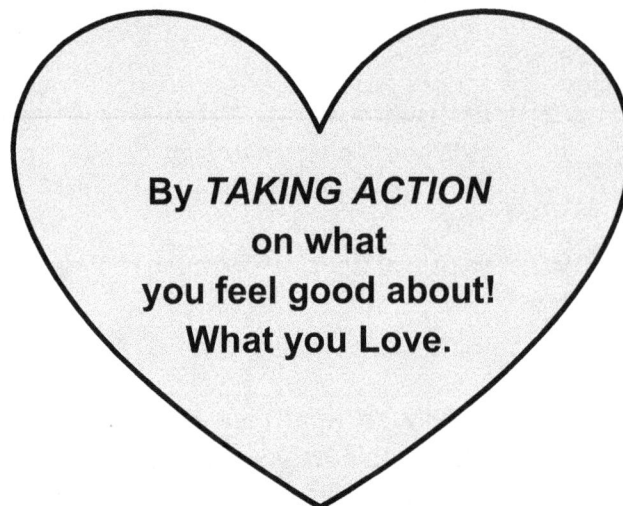

By *TAKING ACTION*
on what
you feel good about!
What you Love.

How Do You Uncover the Information Your Heart is Storing for You?

By recalling memories of what you loved before becoming an adult.

The young part of you or your inner child, holds the seeds of your true authentic self. Keep in mind that you are connecting with the *feelings* that arise as you recall this part of your past.

∞

Try This: Keep a journal of your daydreams. Oftentimes, we fantasize about what makes us feel good. Look for common themes that will reveal your Heart's desires.

∞

Think about this! Why is it that Heart disease is on the rise? Why are we so afraid of our feelings that we *medicate before we investigate* our feeling response to certain situations? Being honest about what is important to you will clear the Heart of energy blockages, affecting not only your ability to manifest, but also the physical health of your Heart.

∞

Connect with your Heart today and make way for manifesting *straight from the Heart!*

⌗ 7 *KNOW YOUR MIND*

"Most folks are as happy as
they make up their Minds to be."

~Abraham Lincoln

The Mind is complex and, at times, may feel like a separate identity as it appears to have its own beliefs on how your life should be lived.

The Mind has a strong will to live and can "chatter" within you constantly to ensure its survival. If you listen, you will notice much of this Mind chatter is fear-based and always on the lookout for danger. It carefully scans the past and future to look for ways to adapt, in order to keep you safe.

> **The most important thing to remember**
> **about the Mind is**
> **that it is changeable!**

How Do You Get To Know Your Mind?

OBSERVE YOUR HABITS AND ROUTINES

Your Mind is like a computer and has a natural ability to store and recall tremendous amounts of information about your life's experiences, how you reacted to events and what compensations (habits) you made to survive. These habits/routines can be changed once you have identified them. Then you can begin replacing them using the information you received working with Body, Soul and Heart. You may be surprised to find out that…

You are not who you think you are!

Try This: Create a vision board. Take a large piece of paper or poster board and attach images, words or phrases you feel represent your intentions and the goals you wish to achieve. This is a visual tool which will keep you focused, clear and ultimately connected to your authentic, true self. Display it somewhere where you will be reminded daily of what it represents. This will target the Mind on exactly what you wish to manifest.

IMPORTANT! The Mind's job is to *collect* the information you have gathered working with your Body, Soul and Heart by *receiving, cataloging, organizing and distributing* the incoming information. This information will then be available for taking action and manifesting your desires.

The Mind does not create new knowledge. It feeds back to you that which YOU have provided. *The results of your manifestation will be directly connected to the clarity of the information that is contained within your Body, Soul and Heart.*

∞

There is a saying in the computer world, *"Garbage In, Garbage Out."* Think of the subconscious/conscious Mind like a computer and your thoughts/feelings are the data. If you input corrupted data, the resulting manifestation will be tainted.

∞

Let's review the lessons of *Body, Soul and Heart* so that you are completely ready when you activate the Mind's ability.

Did you identify?
1. At least one imbalance in your Body and what it is communicating to you?
2. The Archetype, Tone, Color and Feeling, connected to what your Soul wants to manifest?
3. A memory from childhood that indicated to you one of your Heart's desires?
4. An action to take based on what you learned?

WHEN YOU TAKE CARE OF YOURSELF...

THE UNIVERSE WILL TAKE CARE OF YOU!

KNOW THYSELF

****

"I am still learning."

~Michelangelo

****

Keep in mind, learning about YOU lasts a lifetime. As you purify your *Soul, Body, Heart and Mind*, you will discover that your ability to manifest becomes more accurate and in alignment with what you envision for yourself and for the world.

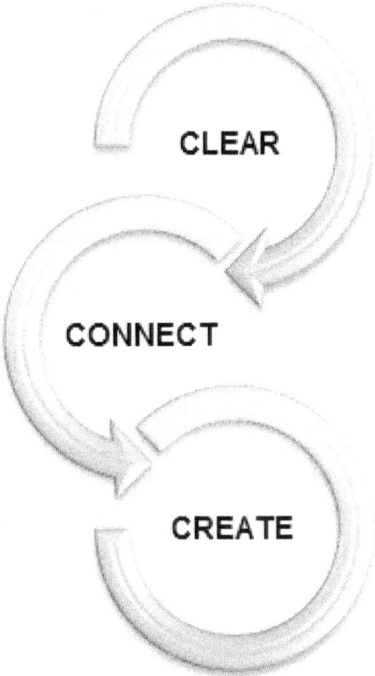

CLEAR

CONNECT

CREATE

****Clear* the imbalances   **Connect* with the Universe   **Create* the life you dream of for yourself and for the world.**

The Divine desires to co-create with you and has provided all you need to live a life of joy and to create positively in the world.

ALL TOGETHER NOW....SAY THANK YOU!

During a session with a client, we were discussing the real and practical value of expressing gratitude. Feeling thankful is critically important when using the Laws of Attraction. In a moment of clarity she said:

"The manifesting process is not complete
until you give gratitude back for what you have received."

Yes! And this explains why sometimes you may feel as if you are not getting what you want or are doing something wrong. It is not that at all. Each of us thrives when appreciation is expressed. It completes the circle of giving/receiving and builds energy for the next manifestation.

When we actively co-create with the Universe, what we offer in exchange for the ability to manifest is the *feeling of gratitude*. This is what the Universal energy flourishes on. By genuinely feeling and expressing thankfulness and love, the Universe will continue to respond to you by sending more of its ever-abundant energy enabling you to continue co-creating.

This is an essential part of being in partnership with the Divine. Simply put, it is good manners and builds energy for the next manifestation process.

*

The *Seven Keys to Effortless Living* are much more than a trend or what is currently popular. The Keys have been within YOU and all of humanity since the beginning of time.

Now, more than at any other moment in history, it is vital that we realize our individual and collective power for manifesting a loving world.

The Universe has provided you with the Keys so that you may create the life of your dreams and inspire others to do the same. When you use each of the Seven Keys *together,* you will unlock the door to manifesting your Dreams and Goals!

> ## NOW GO AND MANIFEST THAT!!

SECTION 3

FOLLOW THE FUN

☼ ARE WE
HAVING FUN YET?

Everyone wants to have fun. Right? Having fun should be easy. Simply do what makes you happy. It is one of the most natural experiences you can have and yet so many suffer from being disconnected from joy and fun in life.

Children frequently have fun because it is encouraged and seen as a necessary part of development. Even animals will spontaneously play throughout the day. Both children and animals have an instinct that directs them to include fun as part of their daily activities. As we grow older, we are conditioned out of this natural attitude.

As adults, we underestimate the importance of having fun has on nourishing the Soul, Body, Heart and Mind. Why? Having fun can be perceived as less important than earning a living and being responsible. Actually, in order to sustain the energy to work, you need to recharge yourself with fun filled activities.

☼FUN AND YOUR HEALTH

It is as simple as:

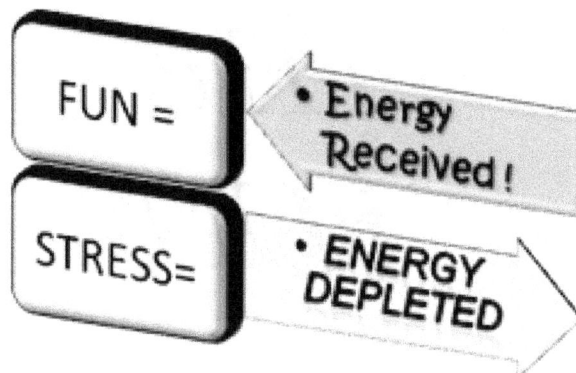

FUN = • Energy Received!

STRESS= • ENERGY DEPLETED

Too much stress has contributed to a serious decline in the overall health of our nation, as evidenced in an increase in drug use, obesity, alcoholism, etc. If we truly felt a continuous presence of joy in our lives, we would not feel the need to use addictive substances or engage in destructive behaviors.

It becomes ever more important, as stress levels continue to rise, to include some experiences of fun, such as laughing or being playful every day.

*

When you experience more stress than fun, the consequences are felt immediately and can have lasting effects, such as:

*Depression   *Fatigue
*Weight Gain   *Sleep Disorders
*Premature Aging *Panic Attacks
*Illness   *Skin Eruptions

The absence of fun has an effect on your Body/Mind connection and…

THE BODY/MIND CONNECTION DIRECTS YOUR HEALTH.

As discussed in the section, *Feel Your Feelings*, stress relieving experiences are different for men and women. Men need to release testosterone and should engage in active, problem solving tasks, whereas women need to release oxytocin through nurturing, giving and time suspended activities.

WHAT DOES IT MEAN TO "FOLLOW THE FUN?"

While researching this book, I discovered my own conditioned response of replacing *"Yes"* with *"No."* An event was being held that I was immediately excited to attend. My first thought was, *"Oh what fun"* and then seconds later my mind started to create reasons why I could not attend. Once I recognized this negative thought process, I decided to see what would happen if I followed my first impulse which was, *"Oh what fun!"* I asked:

"What would
happen
if I
FOLLOWED THE FUN?"

As it turned out, every one of my objections did not materialize. The entire experience was easy and filled with amazing synchronicities which seemed to build upon themselves once the momentum started. It was one fun experience followed by another that I will never forget. Had I listen to my initial objections, I would not have been in the Fun Frequency which connected me to the continuous flow of synchronicities. It was an exciting day that illustrated perfectly what happens when you FOLLOW THE FUN.

HOW TO DO IT. I had to recognize my habitual thought pattern of saying *"No"* to fun. Then I had to take action to change it.

ACTION AND FOLLOW THROUGH are two very important steps to shifting any programmed thought pattern.

It takes time and consistency to change any habit that has been with you for a while but remember:

HABITS

CAN

CHANGE

They are NOT
a permanent part of who you are!

☼ *TIMES WE*
ARE LIVING IN

There is a lot of anxiety and uncertainty in the world today. NOW, more than ever, it is necessary to include regular fun activities as part of your daily life. By doing so, you ***increase your energy and decrease tension.***

Undoubtedly, our world and the structures that have sustained us are in the middle of a great transformation ***AND SO ARE YOU!***

"*In these uncertain times*" is a phrase we commonly hear a lot now, but it does not mean all changes are negative.

During any transformation, there is the unknown and this creates doubt and anxiety. However, *simultaneously, there also exists an opportunity to experience the innate power you have to create positive, joyful change*.

KEEP IN MIND: All change does not have to include chaos.

> **The key to navigating change
> is to experience a continuance of
> GOOD FEELING
> as often as you are able.**

*

The Fun Frequency. When you are feeling joyful or in the *Fun Frequency*, you are literally outside of the challenging reality everyone else is experiencing. Because of your action *to have fun in spite of what is going on around you*, you separate yourself from the effects of negativity.

NOW is exactly the time we need to understand the value of having steady experiences of fun and joy in our lives. Here are some observations to keep in mind:

- Fear constricts and diminishes your ability to receive energy.

- When you are feeling fear, you are unable to connect to hope and the ability to initiate change.

- When you learn to *Follow the Fun*, any adjustment you make reflects that positive energy.

- Positive energy attracts to you what you desire.

- When you *Follow the Fun,* you feel light, hopeful and you become more self-reliant. You are more open to manipulation if you are living in the restrictive energy of fear.

- Self-reliant fun means that you are creating energy and excitement from within yourself and with your connection to the ever-abundant Universe. When you depend on someone or something else to have fun, you diminish your power and your ability to create.

- When you generate fun for yourself, it adds to your personal supply of energy that can improve your health, enhance your mood, and can inspire others to make positive changes in their lives.

☀ *WHY FUN IS FUN-DAMENTALLY IMPORTANT*

When you are feeling good and in the Fun Frequency, you are in direct contact with the infinitely abundant energy of the Universe. This energy is always available to you and appears as synchronicities and ultimately,

> **THE POWER TO MANIFEST
> WHAT YOU WANT!**

These Universal energies are accessible through the experience of <u>feeling</u>. When you are feeling good, you are able to utilize this positive energy to its full potential.

> **Negative feelings
> limit your access to this energy.**

How to Work with the Fun Frequency
In earlier chapters we identified the 7 Keys as:
1. *Be Yourself*
2. *Feel Your Feelings*
3. *Be Happy*
4. *Soul* (receives guidance from the Universe)
5. *Body* (receives Soul guidance and stores it)
6. *Heart* (translates guidance into hopes, dreams)
7. *Mind* (organizes dreams into action)

They are an integral part of how the Universe flows energy through you. As you remove the blocks in these areas and restore their original purpose (as stated above), you will clear the way for the Fun Frequency to connect directly to you. This will result in continuous, synchronistic experiences that lead straight to what you want to manifest.

AND REMEMBER

*It is the Love Frequency
that binds the good feelings together
into a focused creative force.*

Think Of It Like This:
The stronger your vibration of fun is broadcasting, *the more synchronicities you will attract, which results in an increase in your ability to manifest.*

> *Everyday, have fun so that you may interact directly
> with the Fun Frequency AND
> become a co-creator with the Universe in manifesting!*

☀ *LET'S DEFINE FUN*

What Is It? What Does It Feel Like?

> Webster Dictionary defines Fun as:

          1. Something that provides mirth or amusement
          2. Enjoyment or playfulness

Most of us would define fun as a happy emotional state, when you are doing, experiencing, or feeling something pleasing.

    ✓ It can feel uplifting, make you laugh.
    ✓ Fun is light, buoyant and bouncy.
    ✓ Fun is enjoyable and something you want to continue feeling.

Typically, we think of fun as being connected to an experience outside of ourselves, such as an event, the purchase of something special, perhaps taking a vacation or going to an amusement park. These examples are fun, but are based on generating a situation outside of you, sometimes dependent on money, another person or group of people. This is *conditional fun*, which is based on an external experience to stimulate the fun response.

The type of fun I am describing is internal. One based only on *you* to determine if you will have fun or not. It is a conscious choice. This type of fun or joy is the most powerful because it is self-generated. If you are able to connect with this emotional and mental state AT WILL, then wherever you are or whatever is happening to you, YOU can decide to enjoy the experience or not.

This Is A Very Empowering Way
To Live Your Life!

☀ HOW SHOULD FUN FEEL IN THE BODY?

🔥 Fun is feeling you can be and express yourself without fear of rejection.

🔥 Fun uplifts people and can make it safe for them to be their authentic selves.

🔥 Fun feels good because you are releasing endorphins into the body.

⚘ Fun is the feeling that connects you to the Universe.

⚘ Fun is just that…fun. Even human love can be painful, but fun is only FUN.

⚘ Fun is an uncomplicated emotion. It is what it is.

⚘ Fun is an effervescent energy and lifts your Soul, Body, Heart and Mind. When you feel light, you are able to access the ever-abundant Universal energies.

⚘ The absence of fun is heavy and weighted. It is the inability to change.

⚘ Fun is light and enables you to adapt effortlessly.

⚘ Fun has to be a true, authentic fun. It cannot be forced through the manipulation of Soul, Body, Heart and Mind as when using drugs, alcohol or connected to any other addiction.

⚘ Fun should benefit you, those you connect with and be good for the world.

*

Keep In Mind: Advertisers count on you believing that you cannot have fun without their product or service. This is manipulation. You may feel good temporarily by buying products or services, but eventually the feeling diminishes because it was dependent on something external.

> *Material things*
>
> *cannot provide you*
>
> *with fun unless you*
>
> *first have the feeling.*

☀ *THE FUN FUND*

> **IMAGINE THAT THERE ARE TWO LARGE CONTAINERS.**

One is labeled *Stress Fund*

and the other is labeled *Fun Fund*.

When you experience stress, your body responds by drawing energy from your life force to sustain you. This energy can either be drawn from an accumulation of positive experiences that have benefited the body (Fun Fund) or directly from the body itself (Stress Fund), which may lead to a degeneration of health.

When you have accumulated enough experiences that are positive, your body instinctively knows it has the vitality to handle any stressful situation...*it will not take energy from your life force, your body and specifically your adrenal glands to handle the circumstance.*

The more fun you have, the more energy you have to create what you desire. When you experience fun and add that energy to the Fun Fund, it is like adding money to your bank account. It will flourish as long as you continue to supply it with fun.

If you add tension to the Stress Fund, it draws energy directly from your body releasing stress related hormones and causing physical and mental health problems that will continue the downward cycle of generating more stress. *Not the way you want to live!*

AFFECTS OF FUN

Fun in the SOUL means knowing that you are an important part of the Universe. You matter! You are special and can contribute your unique talents to creating a better world. If you understand this about yourself, then you will not expect people, places or purchases to fulfill you.

Fun in the BODY is health. Even if you are ill, you can still choose to have moments of fun, to laugh and enjoy yourself. When you do this, you add energy to the Fun Fund and aid your body in recovering faster.

Fun in the HEART. The Heart is where the Soul stores knowledge from the Universe about your true purpose. Your hopes, wishes and dreams will reveal this to you. Your Heart asks of you,

> *"What is your hope for fun in your life?*
> *"What is you wish for fun in your life?"*
> *"What is your dream for fun in your life?"*

The Heart does not come into life sad. It seeks a deeper, more fulfilling connection with the Divine Universe, which is accessible though joy.

> The Divine is LOVE. All creation
> emanates from this impulse of love,
> which you experience as joy and fun.

Being a co-creative partner with the Divine, means for you to embody the same loving, creative energy. This enables you to use the Laws of Attraction to direct your manifestations.

Fun in the MIND. The mind organizes the information from the Soul, Body and Heart into actionable steps. If you believe that fun is selfish or a waste of time, then your Mind will instruct you to not participate. If you begin to change that programming, even just a little, then anytime you encounter something fun you will not immediately reject it, but will eventually embrace the opportunity.

✸THE KEY IS TO CELEBRATE

Several years ago, I saw an interview with an amazing child named Mattie Stepanek. Mattie had a rare disease that had also claimed the life of his other siblings. He had fought many health battles in his short 14 years and when asked what he did after each time he nearly died, he said,

"I celebrate."

When you celebrate, it immediately uplifts your emotional state releasing calming hormones. This results in an increase in energy, balanced body, better ability to solve problems and a positive outlook.

All Of Which Connects You To The Fun Frequency
And Synchronicities That Give You The Power To Manifest!

When you:

> ➤ Celebrate both big and ordinary events,
> ➤ Have an attitude of gratitude,
> ➤ Consciously choose to live life appreciatively,

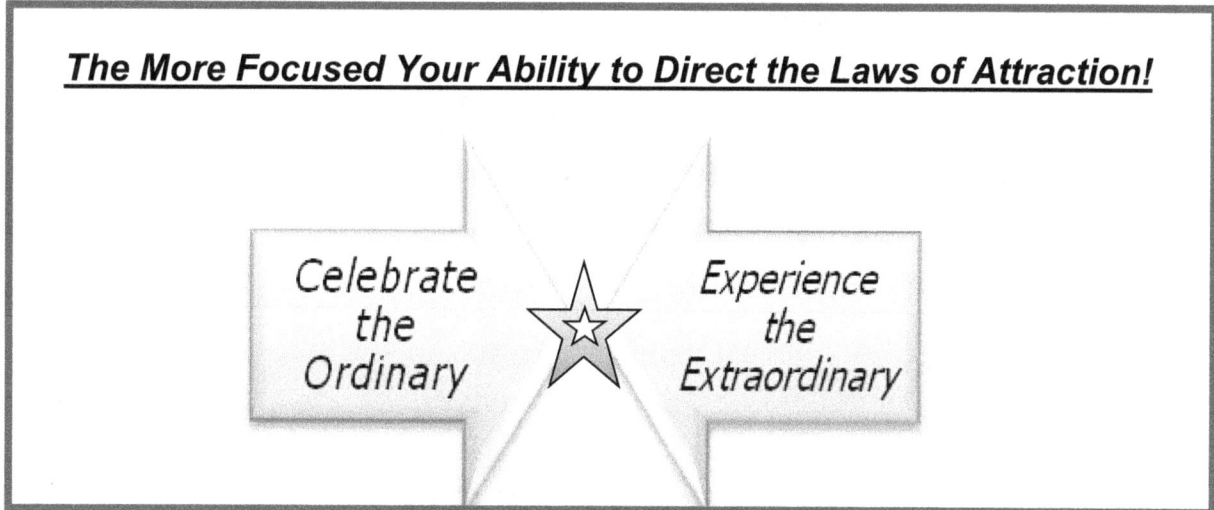

The More Focused Your Ability to Direct the Laws of Attraction!

Celebrate the Ordinary ✰ Experience the Extraordinary

---

*

For more about this inspiring little boy visit: **www.mattieonline.com**

☀BENEFITS OF FUN

✓ Decreases harmful effects of stress

✓ Lowers blood pressure

✓ Reduces aches and pains

✓ Produces more efficient flow of energy through the body

✓ Enhances feelings of optimism

✓ Helps you problem solve

✓ Better able to recognize synchronicities and effectively interact with them

✓ Manifest and use the Laws of Attraction

✓ Be more focused

✓ Improve concentration

✓ Enjoy sexual vitality

✓ Feel connected to creativity

✓ Sense of belonging/no isolation

✓ Improves health

✓ Enhances restorative sleep

✓ Body utilizes nutrition more effectively

✓ Greater intake of oxygen, which is the body's connection to the Universe

✓ Fun is infectious and will positively affect those around you

✓ When two or more are gathered in fun, it has the potential to change people, circumstances, and events on the planet

✓ Release stress reducing hormones

☀THE POWER OF FUN
TO CREATE
A BETTER WORLD

When you are having fun and feeling joyful, you are lifting your Soul, Body, Heart, and Mind (Fundamental Four) out of the box of consensus reality.

When you are connected to this energy, you are also connected to the power of your pure, creative potential.

When you are interacting with your personal creativity, you can manifest more specifically what you want.

When this is happening for you in a regular and meaningful way, it models for others what is possible.

When others see the results in your life created by having fun, they too will feel inspired to connect to this energy within themselves. This will have a domino effect on those they encounter and, in turn, will have a positive influence on the world.

When you are in the Fun Frequency, you are connected to inspiration, the source of all ideas, synchronicity, and manifestation. This combination allows you to bring forth solutions that can benefit your life and, in turn, benefit anyone you come in contact with.

Example:

My Conscious Decision to Connect to Fun is:

Enabling me to lift myself out of melancholy and write the book you are now reading.
After reading this book, you may feel inspired to make changes in your life.
That in turn will affect others and contribute to creating a better world.

UNIVERSE

YOU HAVING FUN!

When you are having Fun, you are connecting and sharing energy with the Universe that allows you to manifest and be a true *Universal co-creator!*

☼FUN AND MONEY

Now, this is an important chapter! With so many changes constantly happening in our economy, we all need to know how to create and sustain sources of income that support our lives.

It is hard to make money or see the opportunities when you are limited by fear. Fear constricts. When your body is in the flight or fight response, you draw your energy inward, compromising your ability to breathe, and become ready to fight and/or ready to run.

Fun, on the other hand, is an expansive energy. When you are having fun and feeling joy, your energy and heart rate increase, and you receive more oxygen, which contributes to a heightened state of awareness where you can *work directly with the Laws of Attraction.* In this state, all things are possible, because you have removed yourself from the lower frequency or density that most everyone else is living in.

What are the Laws of Attraction?
What you *think, feel, visualize, and intend* is what you will attract to you. Therefore, when you are in a *fun, happy* state of mind, you are interacting directly with the energies that allow for the manifestation of what you desire.

☆*TRUE STORY*: I decided to test the theory of *Follow the Fun* by purchasing concert tickets. This was a leap of faith *which is also what Neptune in Pisces represents.*

I knew that having something fun to look forward to should connect my energy, *in present time*, to the Fun Frequency, where I would eventually experience a synchronicity that would attract the money to me.

The question was:

> Would the Universe respond to my decision
> to have fun, *in the future,* if,
> IN THE MOMENT, I was feeling fear?

Two weeks after purchasing the tickets, I received unexpected monetary gifts which equaled double of what the tickets cost. The Universe increased my abundance and proved that:

```
┌─────────────────────────────┐
│     FOLLOWING THE FUN       │
│       IS SUPPORTED          │
│      BY THE UNIVERSE!!      │
└─────────────────────────────┘
```

☀ *WHERE TO BEGIN?*

☼ Think of the moment just before you open a gift; the feelings of anticipation, excitement, wonder, hope. This is where the energy of fun lives.

☼ Try new experiences that connect you to discovery, being curious, adventure and exploration.

☼ Do you replace a gut level *"Yes"* response with *"No"* or create reasons why you cannot do something? You cannot change a behavior until you become aware that you are doing it.

☼ Observe the next time you are happy. Where in your body do you feel it? Stomach, heart, legs? When you identify where your body naturally feels the energy of fun, you can place your hands/attention there when you are sad, angry, etc. and reconnect with the energy/experience of fun.

☼ Be gentle with yourself. It may take some time to change the lifetime habits that you have established. Begin with simple, fun things to do 1 to 2 times each week. Like exercise, *it takes time to teach yourself to be able to handle the energy of fun.*

☼ Use exercise to increase mood elevating endorphins. You will feel a heightened state of energy. When you feel good you are able to interact directly with the Fun Frequency and draw forth synchronistic experiences.

☼ Smile even if you do not mean it. The body recognizes smiling as positive and will respond with the proper biological release of mood enhancing hormones.

☼ If you substituted one fun thought for every limiting thought, you can completely change your life.

KEEP IN MIND!

- When your Fun Fund is filled with positive energy, problem solving is easier.

- There are anti-aging benefits when you are in the Fun Frequency.

- Fun supports your life experience and makes you stronger, whereas fear takes your energy.

- Fun is infectious. You can inspire others by having fun yourself.

- It is never too late to celebrate.

- It is easy to make an acquaintance feel good. Your true goal is to inspire and energize your immediate relationships with positive energy. When this is achieved, the bond of love is strengthened even if the relationship has been stressed.

- Feelings are embedded in DNA and are passed on to future generations.

- How others feel about you is your true legacy. Will people remember feeling happy, inspired and joyful around you or not?

- Feeling good invigorates you and enables you to see more options.

- Fun boosts the vitality of your immune system.

- Good feelings create physical energy.

MOST IMPORTANT OF ALL

Fun gives you access to
the *Love Frequency*
where all energies emanate from.

This frequency powers and binds
the Universal energies
and is ever abundant and
ready for your participation.

SECTION 4

HOW MAY
I
SERVE LOVE?

FINAL THOUGHTS

We stand on the threshold of a very exhilarating change. As Neptune continues its sojourn through Pisces over the next fourteen years, and the effects of the Galactic alignment are made real, we will be given the opportunity to transform as never before. Exactly what each of us does with this opportunity remains to be seen. The true destiny for mankind has always been to be in a co-creative partnership with the Divine in a vast universe of possibility.

Preparing yourself for this begins now. The coming Love Wave starts a process of shedding that which no longer serves the higher calling of love. Ask yourself if you are living the full potential of love in your life. Are you in the right relationship? Do you feel aligned with your authentic self in whatever work or service you do? Have you said what you need to say to those in your life? Remember, *there is only love.* Even the root of fear is designed to protect you from harm. It is meant to increase your awareness so that you will be safe. Fear's objective is ultimately to keep that which the Divine loves, YOU, protected at all times.

One Final Suggestion.

When you feel stuck or are unable to find resolve or understanding, ask of the Divine Universe:

HOW MAY I SERVE LOVE?

When you pose this question, you are asking for a response from the highest source possible. It will not include man-made, limited solutions. The answer will be all inclusive with the highest good considered and in fact, may surprise you in the illogical solution it provides. Remember, it is the pure energy of Love at work for your benefit!

If you doubt the answer than apply the questions of discernment:

❖ *IS THIS FACTUAL?*
❖ *IS THIS PRACTICAL?*
❖ *IS THIS LOVING?*

I have asked myself this question when I felt unable to find a solution. I was shocked by the synchronicities that resulted such as:

- Friends contacting me after long separations
- Spontaneous communications just to say, "I Love you"
- Random appearance of phone numbers, emails, addresses of lost connections
- Communications from long lost friends with amends for past behaviors

When we seek out Love Solutions that benefit everyone, in return, we receive greater love experiences for ourselves.

Neptune in Pisces asks that we adjust our thinking towards solutions that are all inclusive.

Keep working on clearing your Soul, Body, Heart and Mind to prepare for the coming changes. One person really can make a difference. By eliminating the stresses in your body, you make yourself ready to receive and uncover the blueprint for your Divine evolution. As you become better able to sustain the Love Frequency inside you, you will radiate this love to those in your life and in your world. As they see the changes in you, it will inspire them to ask, *"With so many difficulties going on in the world, how is it that you are feeling good, looking great and in such a positive mood?"*

Remember, with the time distortions of Neptune in Pisces, healing does not have to take a long time or require years in self-reflection. Pay attention, be willing to take action at the right time and ask:

HOW MAY I SERVE LOVE?

SUSAN'S STORY

I wrote this book to heal myself. Although my intuitive abilities are of help to others, it has been physically and mentally challenging for me to achieve balance. I have frequently succumbed to negative, hopeless thinking. My wiser self has always known that the purpose of life is to experience giving and receiving love, to feel joy and have fun. However, I had been unable to achieve this and it has had a profound ill effect on my health. The imbalance between what I know and what I had been able to achieve left me feeling deeply depressed. *"Why am I like this?"* was constantly on my mind and I was determined to understand the origin of the pain.

I would often declare, *"I want to have fun!"*, but just the opposite would happen manifesting in overwhelming, stressful situations that left me sick and depleted of energy. Eventually, I discovered a deep, ancestral family belief pattern that *fun was not safe and that I was not deserving of the happiness I perceived in others.*

I knew my core beliefs had to be challenged, so I started to investigate what would ACTUALLY happen if I let myself have fun and enjoy life. I have to honestly tell you that many times, as I experienced fun, another chaotic event or illness would befall me soon afterwards. I was stunned as to how REAL this belief seemed, as it actualized itself in my life. So I decided to investigate the FACTS of the belief and not the feeling. This resulted in the revelation of the **Seven Keys to Effortless Living** and an understanding of how the *Soul, Body, Heart* and *Mind* (especially the Body/Mind connection) affect how we experience reality.

From my work, I know that the Divine Universe creates only in *wholeness* and that it is we who believe we are separate from this unity. Understanding this made me certain that my sensitivities were purposeful and not meant to cause suffering. They do give me the unique talent of being able to understand the deep hidden information submerged within the collective unconscious.

Through my direct experience and the resulting ill affects upon my body, I discovered that there is an innate system of health and wholeness that has always been within us. Remember, we are created in Divine wholeness and,

THE DIVINE DOES NOT LEAVE US WITHOUT SOLUTIONS

In fact, on some level, there was never an imbalance to begin with, only our unwillingness to believe that AT ALL TIMES we are loved, supported and provided for.

Since the belief that Fun equals danger is deep in my ancestral family patterning, it requires me to continually challenge my ability to create fun minus the chaos. As I continue to contribute to the Fun Fund, the presence of joy in my life is now more real than previously experienced. My physical and mental health is consistently more balanced, and I am able to experience deeper, more meaningful connections. This is proof to me that we were always intended to be joyful and fun loving as an expression of our true, Divine, authentic selves.

I KNOW this is possible for you. Even if you are not experiencing ill health as a symptom of the lack of fun, you can use my example to know that:

Health   Finances   Enjoying Life   Feeling Safe   Being Happy

are possible
RIGHT NOW,
TODAY in your life.

We are in an unprecedented time of transformation that will require you to pay attention like never before. Chaos and uncertainty is a natural part of any change but by following the techniques in this book you will be able to handle the new experiences. It is now necessary to embrace this information and any other you find helps you to heal and restore yourself to the authentic, natural, beautiful person you are and have every right to be.

Know that no matter what happens, **Love Is Always Stronger** and for the first time, as the boy Ratyja said in the dream "since the first release of creation", we have the opportunity to prepare ourselves, families, friends and the world to be ready to receive the joy Divine Love offers and to use that energy to co-create our Dreams and manifest our Goals!

Susan Elizabeth Espinosa
October 24, 2012
Dream and Goal For It®
www.DreamandGoalForIt.com

SECTION 5

REFERENCES
&
ADDITIONAL
INFORMATION

LET'S REVIEW AND SUMMARIZE

WHAT EACH KEY REPRESENTS

AND HOW TO ACCESS IT

****

KEY 1 – BE YOURSELF

❖ Eliminate past conditioning.

❖ Connect with a childhood memory you enjoyed.

❖ Incorporate that memory into your life today. Make it real.

KEY 2 – FEEL YOUR FEELINGS

❖ They are your natural guidance system.

❖ Do not suppress your feelings. It creates Body imbalances.

❖ The Universe responds to your feeling and tracks your manifestation back to you like a homing beacon.

KEY 3 – BE HAPPY

❖ Being happy is your natural state of being and is available to you at all times.

❖ Try not to worry as it depletes your energy for manifesting.

❖ Being happy is what you want to feel *before* you work with the Laws of Attraction.

KEY 4 – SOUL

❖ When you are being yourself, Key 1, you are in direct alignment with your Soul.

❖ Soul communicates through archetype, tone, color and feeling.

❖ You can also use archetype, tone, color and feeling to create a language in which to have a direct dialogue with your Soul, Body, Heart and Mind.

KEY 5 – BODY

❖ Learn the Soul/Body language and understand the meaning of your aches, pains and illness.

❖ The Body does not know the difference between what is real or imagined.

❖ Make sure your thoughts are positive and energy producing and your body will respond in kind.

KEY 6 – HEART

❖ Recall memories of what you loved before becoming an adult.

❖ Take action on what you feel good about.

❖ Keep a journal of your daydreams.

KEY 7 – MIND

❖ Know that the mind is changeable. You are not fixed to a particular way of thinking or behaving.

❖ Observe your habits and routines and know that they too are changeable.

❖ Create a vision board with images of your authentic self. This will target the mind on exactly what you want to achieve.

A FEW SOUL MEANINGS FOR YOUR BODY

FEET: Foundation. Keeps you grounded. Moves you in a direction whether forward, backward or sideways in your life

LEGS: Move you forward. Supports your direction.

KNEES: Surrender

HIPS: Personal identity

STOMACH: Home

LUNGS: Where the Divine enters in the form of breath

KIDNEYS: Fear

BREASTS: Nurturing, mother

SHOULDERS: Responsibility, weight you bare

ARMS: Reach forward in life

BACK: Support systems, often times financial

LOWER BACK: Childhood support systems

THROAT: Ability to communicate

For a more extensive list, check out Louise Hay's book, _Heal Your Body._

SUGGESTED READING

Gregg Braden

Research into the healing power of feelings

Divine Matrix

www.greggbraden.com

Dr. Masura Emoto

How words change the molecular structure of water

Messages in the Water

www.masaru-emoto.net

Dr. John Gray

Understanding hormonal affects in men and women

Venus on Fire, Mars on Ice

www.marsvenus.com

Louise Hay

Connection between Body and Mind

Heal Your Body

www.louisehay.com

Drunvalo Melchizedek

Love, Truth, Beauty, Trust, Harmony, Peace

The Ancient Secret of the Flower of Life

www.drunvalo.net

Mattie Stepanek

"I celebrate"

Heart Songs

www.mattieonline.com

**

EXTRA

Catherine Ponder

The Prospering Power of Love

catherineponder.wwwhubs.com

James Redfield

How to work with the energy of synchronicity

The Celestine Prophecy Series

www.celestinevision.com

DREAM AND GOAL FOR IT.COM

Susan Elizabeth Espinosa is natural born intuitive, life coach, visionary artist and author. Her unique abilities allow her to see deep into the patterns of Cause and Effect. This allows her clients the rare experience of *previewing* how decisions made today will affect the future. This transformational information results in meaningful spiritual insights and real, practical advice.

Since 1994, Susan has been teaching and sharing her gifts with people from all over the world including celebrities, philanthropists, political influencers, authors, professionals and seekers of truth in all faiths and beliefs. She is the intuitive coach for other intuitive professionals.

She is available for one on one life coaching consultations and group events.

To contact Susan:

Website: www.DreamandGoalForIt.com

Phone: (818) 377-5196

Email: susan@dreamandgoalforit.com